Rooting for Humanity

for Mary Alice Johnston*
who describes our life together as
"Sixty-two years of Holy Deadlock"

*Mary Alice Johnston also made the cover photograph
and a book of her classic photographs of Paris after the war
is slated for publication by Western Eye Press.

Rooting
for
Humanity

poems

Richard Johnston

WESTERN EYE PRESS
2010

This book is published by
WESTERN EYE PRESS,
a small independent publisher
(very small, and very independent)
with a home base in the Colorado
Rockies and an office in Sedona
Arizona, using an innovative
on-demand publishing service,
createspace.com.
ROOTING FOR HUMANITY
is also available as an eBook
in various formats.

Western Eye Press
P O Box 1008
Sedona, Arizona 86339
1 800 333 5178
www.WesternEyePress.com

First edition, 2010:
ISBN-13   978-0-941283-25-0
electronic or eBook edition:
ISBN-13   978-0-941283-26-7

Rooting for Humanity

Rooting for Humanity

From life's first organic cell
through random atom collocations
that peopled all existing nations
to Hiroshima's Nuclear Hell
we would be wise to recognize
that natural life was given birth
on our exploded star of planet
through roots in Mother Earth

PART ONE

Awakenings

Diurnal Drama

Pink blushes of light
in the eastern sky
ripple through bare trees
across my front yard
tidal waves of time
flowing on set while
atop a leafless cottonwood
a Towsend's Solitaire
pipes winter on stage

Tick tock of kitchen clock
grappling with eternity
hum of quiet motor
creating its own micro winter
in the arctic depths
of the refrigerator
two alert deer as ushers
watching my unlit window

Fleeting pre-dawn moment
when the revolutionary
faces the firing squad
the new bride snuggles
into warm waiting arms

the condemned prisoner
hears the rustle of harness
on the electric chair
the home-birth baby greets
the world with a lusty cry

What will be the
plot this day
the hero wins
or the hero loses
the director directs
but the audience
chooses the
role I play
on stage today

Will I know
my lines, my cues
the players or their
order of appearance
will the first be Joy
will she be Luck
will she be Grief
hold steady
dawn's curtain
starts to rise
I am ready

Running Free

What do I see on my morning run
when flowers give color to the sun
dancing trees give shape to the west wind's flow
sparkling rocks paint foam on the stream
below the bass-drum bridge
with a beat, beat, beat
alien music of splattering feet
invading the calm of a wild retreat
nearby where half-hidden antelope graze
as mountains sculpt the eastern sky

What in the amorous dawn do I hear
while birds sing love songs
to shy brown deer
and voices of silence
like unspoken prayer
heighten the hush of the cool dry air
and the soaring magic of mountain walls
nature's echoing concert halls
sound out the sweetest siren songs
of druid chants and pagan calls

What do I feel in the gold blue light?
the quickening pulse of a waking world
as mountains doff soft nightcaps
from peaks with crisp white clouds

shadows on the blowing sand
smoke signals of a language
we do not understand
running lines of sacred script
that seem to say to me,
stay within your running pace
look within your psychic space
find within that hallowed place
a way to set your spirit free
Free to be, being free, free to be

Dance of Life

To throw one's mind into the arms
of dancing phantom muses
and acquiesce to all the charms
an exercise that uses dormant
force and slumbering skill
long held beneath convention
but capable of waking still
in a self called to attention
a poetry as yet unheard
like a sudden sweet love potion
a rhythmic wisdom of the word
ballet of graceful motion

The Shape of Freedom

The corrosive magic
of a new Atomic Science
shattering centers of authority
lines of demarcation
separating power of science
from guidance of culture
a cosmic community of being

Claiming privilege
as proud Americans
escaping to the licensed
use of our automobiles
and the unlicensed
permission of our desires
to eat, drink and be happy

Intoxicated by freedom
to pursue the bountiful life
abanoning authority
of restraint and modesty
practicing mutual respect
and common civility
for fellow humans

Open Path

As life rolls by on wheels of chance
with pleasure pain and danger
let all my choices be engaged
with many options open
endowed with danger and romance
and tinged with mystery
behind a psychic curtain
with access points all closed
to those whose goal is to impose
a plan to make life certain

Our Twin Self

Our twin self,
who makes us truly human
ever with us but
elusive to our needs
it hangs out in the garden
and hides among the weeds
or slips into the brain's great malls
where it is hard to find
and doesn't answer cell phone calls
to that solitary realm of mind
it sleeps in little cat naps
resting to keep its poise
even when our conscience
is making lots of noise

The Zen of Memory

To catch a memory passing by
or trying to remember who
however desperately I try
I almost always fail to do
but searching to recall whatnot
some bit of data not selected
long sought and quite by now forgot
comes clearly into memory's ken
in the quick and simple way of Zen
so easy and so unexpected

PART TWO

Life and Love

About Love

Love's not a bargain to be driven
nor a trade to be arranged
it is never something to be given
true love can only be exchanged

For Mary

From charcoal burners in the streets
came roasting chestnut smells
incense for sidewalk bistro seats
where vendors' cries cast magic spells
the river boats that autumn night
were floating free in pools of light
as hand in hand in rapt delight
we walked along the winding Seine
our young hearts gay, our future bright
Paris was sheer heaven then

The Story of Creation

The first by God created
Adam was his name
Adam ate an apple
and put the world to shame
but when he had to grapple
with that which he had wrought
and saw what cause it gave to grieve
he slyly cast about and sought
to blame the whole affair on Eve

So then upon all womankind
an Evil spell was laid
for evermore she was to find
a lowly role to play as maid
and serve as man's caretaker
a troubled trail henceforth to plod
in sorrow thou shalt bring forth children
imposed by God her Maker
to clearly mark her newborn state
a most strange fate to contemplate
Now don't you think that odd
of God ?

Open Heart Therapy

We limit access to our heart
emotional protection for
that vital part of being
insurance against rejection
in deadly fear of freeing
a passage to this trysting place
transcending love and lover
a new dimension of rapport
which could erase existing space
between the self and other

Revelation

Into the deepest deep of sleep
alas, how memory doth creep
in timeless freedom there to find
the close-locked secrets of the mind
and hold them up to fullest view
so we can see ourselves anew
bereft of daytime self-esteem
to face the naked truth of dream
and struggle to unmask life's plot
of what is real and what is not

On Taking

It is no trick to get a knack for taking
childhood Christmas mornings are a start
we claim our right to gifts upon awaking
with little thought for helpful duties
nor feel of need to learn the useful arts
of buying, wrapping, planning or of baking

The whys of rites in which we are partaking
that grown-up fun of sharing can impart
companionship of mutual undertaking
like what we later learn in love
where each of us must come to play a part
if only to conceal a heart that's aching

And finding out at last there's no mistaking
that giving is required to win another's heart
with no resort to trickery or faking
as tricks at Halloween consist in making
(no exchange expected in this festive mart)
just calls to claim our treats for taking

Your love I took as gifts of joy for living
an artless carefree life I thought was smart
and so I take (Face up!) the pain of making
the best of your resolve to live apart

Loom of Life

Time spins our lives in finest threads
and weaves them into tangled skeins
a fateful mix of hopes and dreads
warp and woof of hearts and brains
we think we are the ones who weave
the patterns of our destiny
and often do ourselves deceive
believing that we are free
to form our lives as we would will
unraveling patterns with us still

The fabric of our lives now worn
as time a heavy toll does take
when the dreams we wove are torn
to tattered shreds as we awake
to find the shuttle of the years
flies swiftly leaving little room
for changing doubts and fears
but adversity is a priceless school
and love a powerful mending tool

Land Mines

Soldiers silently probing among
wild flowers for metal bulbs
charged with compressed memories
of hate, revenge, oppression, genocide
planted in the topsoil of history
waiting to blossom as instant death
or be harvested as mutilation
from fields abandoned by war

Battle sites in psychic meadows
of the unsuspecting subconscious
sanctuaries for unmarked spaces
where the surface lightly covers
powerful fragments of past events
sleeping live mines
armed with memories

Potent payload of incomplete
and sensual dreams, desires
unsolved puzzles, unrequited passions
unacknowledged problems
infernal mental machines waiting
to be detonated by a careless-step
or the unthinking grasp
weapons cleverly located in
strategic places by the most elusive
of all adversaries
Ourselves

Attraction

Inner itching of desire
sensuous biology the fuel
arid winds of daily strife
drying the Sybaritic flesh
the smile, the smell, the open look
matches that can light a fire
kindle basic sparks of life
well-spring of intrinsic lust for
pools of pleasure in the dust

If Fish Could Fly

If fish could fly and nest in trees
they might be chased and stung by bees
or snatched by varmints on the ground
or be annoyed by traffic sounds
and take the time to contemplate
that life in water was just great

Limits of change

from bundled bud
a lovely rose like this

as brilliant butterfly
from chrysalis

and so great oak
from acorn comes to be

but nature spoke
and did decree

that creatures such as I
can reach no apogee

apart from what
was always me

A Fire Bell In The Night

Tom Jefferson if you could see
our sad and suffering land
where politics was meant to be
a tool to help us understand
and learn to build foundations
for a fortress of the free
a beacon light for nations

surely you would recognize
the lust for power that fuels
a struggle wherein each one tries
to dominate, as in the duels
beneath the tree of liberty
that marked your days of battle
of slander, lies and calumny
like a Burr beneath your saddle

this lack of trust and bravery
which moved you once to write
of the usage of black slavery
calling for ways we might redeem
the nation's soul in blight
invading sleep and freedom's dream
like a fire bell in the night
as one whose noble words lit fires
that for generations hence
inspired the best in most of us

and whose riddle-laden life
such puzzling signals gave
presiding over troubled times
while sleeping with a slave
fit symbol for our own distress
from history's open grave

Liquidity

Along the Pacific coastline
blood rushing from the heart
tides pulling from under foot
I walk on wet beach sand
feeling insecure upon my
tiny shelf space of planet

Tears of sadness form
salty sea breeze wets my eyes
in failing light of dusk
I step carefully around
gelatinous sea creatures oozing
with the tidal flow like pus
from a recent wound

Wet with sweat from plowing
through spongy sandbanks
I feel an urge to respond to
humidity with retained urine
as if I am part of this biological
ferment of decaying sea life

Seaweed and rotting driftwood
the night air seem one with
my own metabolic functions
warm thick sticky medium
like semen waiting to fertilize
creation of life among dead sea shells

Bathing in warm controlled wetness
marbled hot pool of beach hotel
I think of mother's milk, watching
young women with breasts modeled
like rounded sand hills in swirling tides
tasting salt in my flowing saliva

Frontier Woman

Watching for hostile natives
unremitting work
hemorrhoids, varicose veins
from past pregnancies
lonely, nearest neighbor
a day's horseback ride away

Wife, mother, caretaker
predictable source of cheer
encouragement and hope
stretching the food supply
listening for the sharp
cough in the night
ministering to her children,
husband and animals with
love and homemade medicine

Unsung life of
devotion and courage
"She was a good woman,
we will miss her,"
says the parson
over his Bible
by the solitary gravesite

Photo Synthesis

I took a memory of you
developed it in the
darkroom of loneliness
printing in retrospect
a glossy cover picture
Woman Of My Future

In this jumbled life album
your image synthesizes
the light before and,
shadows after you left
a chiaroscuro sketch of love
as documentary history

Like old sepia prints
of the history museum
where in semi darkness
under the exhibit of
an old Confederate flag
I first kissed you

Amazing Graces

Faith, a slender reed indeed
to change what nature has decreed
by substituting wish for need

Hope is but a futile flight
from daily blight and sorrow
obstructing anything we might
do now to help tomorrow

Charity's for folks below
our norm on whom we may bestow
some gift to make our ego glow

Faithful practice of these graces
admits us to the best of places

Under Control

Birth control
for some a sin to expiate
they hesitate to try it

Girth control
from wide-spread fear
of overweight
we leap on any diet

Mirth control
from deep distrust
of joy sensate
blue laws would deny it

The Utility of Pain

We cling to suffering and pain
(phantoms of times outworn)
the while our mind reverts
to all that which our fears sustain
(shadows over time unborn)
biting the tooth that hurts

Religio Modernus

JESUS in flickering neon
under a luminous cross
shedding light upon the
worship of a congregation
for whom the briefcase
the laptop computer
the cellular telephone
the corporate credit card
the stretch limousine
the jeweled Rolex
the private corporate jet
become sacred symbols
for busisness-inspired
megalithic churches
offering junk food
for the soul

Blind Faith

From spears, clubs and arrows
to atom's nuclear fire
feeding fear of hunger
encouraging desire
for security and conquest
some say it's nature's law

History shows us many means
to these most cherished goals
like peaceful parley, compromise
sailing the treacherous shoals
of habit, custom, fear of change
that hold us all in thrall

A will to kill with conscience clear
some higher cause to celebrate
the love of God and country
shapes culture brick by brick
blind faith provides the mortar
and tries to do the trick

The Cloistered Life

To keep myself safe and secure
I've taken careful measures
vowing always to abjure
a risk to my life treasures
my jewels kept in a strong bank box
my body for example
safely enclosed from hat to sox
in garments plain and ample
my mind relieved of pain and grief
by higher powers above
clothed in that divine belief
that puts my darkest fears to rest
and makes life fit me like a glove
thus have I had the very best
of everything but love

The Power of Words

I am enclosed in
a cage of concepts
invisible bars of my
mindset cell are words
laden through history
with cargos of
specialized meaning

Words carve the contours
of my consciousness
words of comfort and love
words of racism and hate
arrogance of national pride
religious intolerance
ethnic superiority
sexual bigotry
incarcerating imagination

My spirit tries to extricate
and guide me toward a
better fate by opening doors
for which I have no key
converting word-bars of my cell
into the tools to set me free

PART THREE

Nature and Us

Songs of Nature

Sounds of wind in whispering reed
sacraments of nature's creed
engenders peace of mind for me
most restful balm of euphony
that often in the past has brought
my own unburdened world of thought

The Earth Remembers

The ancient earth mocks
the broken plow
the broken dreams
spectors of times past
shattered empires
decaying civilizations
whose molding bones
and crumbling creations are
footprints of history
haunting the fragile moment

Momentos of mortality
scattered about us
on and in the earth
rejoining the womb
from which we sprang
fertilizing future dreams
and the earth remembers
like a broken leg from childhood
returning on rainy days
to nudge the nervous system

The earth remembers
every cut of the forest
scars of burning slash piles
mountain tops blown off
for pleasure and profit

costly cosmetic surgery
every dam, canal, levee
draining natural wetlands
to control nature

The earth remembers
her immune system
resisting invasive forces
slumbering earthquakes
breaking out like a
heavy menstrual flow
of spewing molten lava
unimaginable demolition
while creating new horizons
altered coast lines
changing climate patterns
case historiy of another
fleeting earthling episode

Fate of The Earth

We do not hold the earth in thrall
to serve us as a shopping mall
which some say nature does offend
and could bring earth untimely end
but just to add a note of cheer
for what we might expect anon
indifferent earth will still be here
long after all our kind are gone

Grand Canyon

Workshop of eternity
molded by millennia
into a living tribute to
spirits inhabiting the land
helping the river Colorado
sculpt this sacrarium
for gods of nature

Graphic geo-cardiogram
recording heartbeats
of pulsating nature
sending throughout
earth's forming body
a blood stream of
molten lava flows
raging river floods
and gentle rains

Case study
in the biography
of mother earth
printed in lines of color
on the great pages
of canyon walls
where moving fingers
of light and shadow
trace unforgettable messages
in the hearts of those
who can interpret the language

Boulder Night Skies

From Colorado Flatirons
neighboring mountains
below starlit space in
pine-scented moonlight
a splendor unknown to
less favored places
glimmers of relevance
the immortality of
long-dead stars
lighting our skies,
our hearts, our spirits
glowing nova altars
symbols of Truth
light-miles away
answerable to no
particular faith
no corporeal entities
vast as the unbounded scope
of the human heart
complex as the limitless reaches
of the human brain

Poem For My Grandchildren

This poem is for you
when you were born
you became one of my creditors
from whom I am borrowing
my portion of the earth
with all its riches

Your generation will have
a chance to join the
great explorers of history
discovering new horizons
establishing and sustaining
a constantly changing universe
to break our habit of
spending your children's future

If we can learn to love the earth
our mother who has given birth
to everything we see around
us on our precious plot of ground
and keep it free from trash and neat
help natural cycles to repeat
new growth so we fulfill our dreams
renewing forests fields and streams
perhaps we can return to you
what we have borrowed good as new

Idol Thoughts

In the beginning
was the end
for each beginning
is the end of
a prior beginning
which becomes the
beginning of a
subsequent ending
that closes
a circle of certainty

And circle of certainty
turns to wheel of fate
turns sacred tree to
altar struck in stone
apotheosis of God
flesh of our flesh
bone of our bone
sculpted in marble,
bronze or clay
our Gods begin
and end that way

Old Gods
with great reluctance die
and in their place
indifferent temple of the sky
new Gods spring up
new forms of grace
old idols with a lifted face

Man With Lantern

"How, worthy Sage, can I help?"
"By standing out of my light."
nor fear nor pride dilute
this declaration as
Great Alexander steps aside while
Diogones probes with thought
the dark unfathomed places
searching with flickering lantern
a path that wisdom traces
looking for an honest man
a trait we seldom treasure
nor thing we rush to celebrate
choosing to procrastinate
watching videos replete
with humor, sex and action
diverting call of duty
with infinite distraction
from third-world hunger
pain and early childhood death
from growing migrant camps
escaping real-world suffering
with our channel-changing lamps
fantastic world of wealth extremes
those most diverting scenes
this shadow world of Plato's cave
in pixels on our TV screens

PART FOUR

War and Death

The Love of War

when life grows dull
on farm and field
and a sudden lull
slows business yield
butcher, baker, chief and clerk
scrambling to find some work
spirits sunk in drear morass
poor prospects for the working class
wondering what life is for
a best quick fix is always war
our Manifest Destiny to shoulder
the White Man's Burden
to make a better world
safe for democracy
the game of statesmen
aphrodisiac of politicians
stimulant for the economy
tranquillizer of critical thought
a welcome diversion from
everyday sameness of lives
void of hope or challenge

Song of The Lost Harvest

Young soldiers
planted row on row
best spring seedlings
of a generation
destined never to ripen
nor to bear fruit

White crosses, row on row
blanket miles of rolling hills
and grassy meadows
north of Verdun
marble markers festoon
the quiet splendor of Arlington
and modest inland parks
near Veterans Homes

Muffled drumbeat of
rain on dry soil
to the soughing wind
through wooden crosses
and tangled weeds
moon, sun and stars
cover the lost crop
that will know no harvest

Sacred Symbol

Saluted flag on classroom wall
tool to dupe the kids in school
loyalty to heeding any call
chance to flower in time of war
love of country in the bud
no weeds of negative emotion
fertilizing true devotion for
harvesting of death and blood

Graveyard of Empires

These dark and angry moments
when a nation's heart must weep
lost people turned upon themselves
in a rashness of despair
lacking will to meet the task
for want of savoir faire
and leaders with the guts to ask
that we assume our due
are destined then to sorrow
we kill them and others who
might rise to meet tomorrow

O Kennedys, O Malcom X
O Martin Luther King
O countless sons of Uncle Sam
whose buried bones lie moldering
victims of monumental scam
black hole of soul called Vietnam
and even more repulsive yet
a therapy of shock and awe
to wipe the slate of history
inciting us to just forget
to spend our blood for oil and power
avenging now those shattered towers
where all this foolishness began
that graveyard called Afghanistan

War Against Life

War cries blowing in the wind
energizing the struggle
of science and technology
ranged against
what troubles us
medical bombs attack germs
keeping our species dominant
carbon dioxide feeding
the atmospheric furnace
warming flora and fauna
cross-bred plants and animals
fragile and vulnerable

PART FIVE

Completions

Night Flight

Evening shadows
march across the land
absorbing the horizon
moving the skyline
from nearby mountains
to my front door
threshold of another time
an unexplored frontier
nightfall mantles the world

I am prepared
for a new passage across
the boundaries of time
into the custody
of sheltering darkness
a place called night
with fertile dream beds
where imagination blooms
like flowering plants
in the black light

Intrepid voyager
orbiting inner space
unidentified reality
no workplaces
no calendars
no clocks

no telephones
only the rich emptiness
of my interior world

Panoramic flight
over past prairies
strewn with relics
friendships not returned
promises not kept
truths not spoken
love turned aside
speed and spirit waver

 past subsumes presence
tomorrow is yet to come
to this no man's land
between time zones
the future is yesterday's egg
and tomorrow's sperm
in the womb of night
conceiving promises

Savor the maya of
this time in being
between heartbeats
of eternal rhythms
frozen fraction of forever
pregnant with promise
this mindful moment

new paths to be taken
no time for regret
a new world to waken

Close the door on the day
that night may never end
close the door on the day
let time past flaws emend
as wondrous nature sleeps
in gentle hibernation
let disobedient dreams hold sway
embrace this sweet regeneration

Tea With Thanatos

When Death first calls on me
on that final closing date
I hope that I will be prepared
to pay the mortgage on my fate
and in my house and free so we
can meet and have a chance to find
the time to make a pot of tea
and sit and chat a while if he
is at his ease and so inclined

Before he goes about his task
of doing all the things he must
I want to have a chance to ask
about the views we've come to trust
concerning life beyond the grave
what teachers, preachers, gurus, sages
creating hope that most folks crave
have been propounding through the ages
to dry our tears and calm our fears

Is there the slightest chance I'll ask
at some pause in the conversation
that we will meet another day
I've read about reincarnation
and thought about my Karma count
some say that death pays all our dues
but if I should owe a great amount
what future would I have to lose?

If this a dreamless sleep will be
I'll tell him that is not so strange
and hence will not be new to me
living within this mountain range
a primal place where gods abound
such space as this high valley seems
with peace and beauty all around
in these Elysian Fields we've found
and so have felt scant need for dreams.

Beside Myself

Ours has not been
an easy relationship
not always fully
mindful of each other
enjoying mutual trust

We sought diversion
outside ourselves
in worldly things
in work and play
in the love of power
and the power of love

We immersed ourselves
in the surrogate universe
of electronic media
watching television
a sometimes interesting
substitute for living

Sometimes engrossed
in the lives of others who
won or lost fortunes
the famous and infamous
often spectators
rather than actors
in our own lives

Such a long coexistence
with our beautiful
moments of harmony
and painful periods of
dissention and dissonance
impels integration

We are approaching
now that far horizon
where out long journey ends
as our trail meets the sky
we need to make friends
Myself and I